ANCHOR BOOKS

BLOSSOMING POETS

Edited by

Natalie Catterick

First published in Great Britain in 2004 by
ANCHOR BOOKS
Remus House,
Coltsfoot Drive,
Peterborough, PE2 9JX
Telephone (01733) 898102

All Rights Reserved

Copyright Contributors 2004

SB ISBN 1 84418 360 2

FOREWORD

Anchor Books is a small press, established in 1992, with the aim of promoting readable poetry to as wide an audience as possible.

We hope to establish an outlet for writers of poetry who may have struggled to see their work in print.

The poems presented here have been selected from many entries, and as always editing proved to be a difficult task.

I trust this selection will delight and please the authors and all those who enjoy reading poetry.

Natalie Catterick
Editor

CONTENTS

Killing Nature	Sonya Ogden	1
The Oak Tree	Neil Kelly	2
The Sanctuary	George W Donnellan	3
Cornfield Poppies	Sheila Waller	4
Olivia	Leigh Benton	5
Tulips	Jean V F Tillett	6
The Likely Lady	Stan Whomsley	7
Walk Around	Sharon Fleming	8
John On Saturday	William Hutton	10
The Last Waltz	Eirlys Jones	11
Untitled	E McCanny	12
The World In A Leaf	David Foreman	14
Dawn	J Ellis	15
Butterfall	Thomas Campbell	16
Relaxation	Seamus Harrington	17
These Are The Days In My Garden	James McKay	18
Jobs Worth	J Shires	19
Breakfast	Margaret Kent	20
A Chance To Save Creation	Jason Alexander Nelson Whitehall	21
The Oak Tree Is Crying	John Hoyland	22
Untitled	John Kingston Pool	23
Angel	Malcolm Dexter-Tissington	24
The Blue Veil	Derek Wade	26
My Own Little World	Charlotte Willis	27
Green Fingers?	Gillian Adair	28
The Wood Anemone	Marion Brown	29
Look Into My Garden	C A Walsh	30
A Natural Mirage	Darren Kelly	31
A Gardener's Lament	Uldine F Emmerson	32
Dragonfly	L J Liggett	33
Untitled	Sue Norris	34
The Gardener	Irene Greenan	35
Pendle	Ellen Spiring	36
Flowers	David Williamson	37

Harvest Time	Joan-Ing Reed	38
A Fairyland of Bliss	Iorwerth Thomas (Miner's Poet)	39
Silent Dream	Dorothy Ellis	40
Springtime	Jim Cruickshank	41
My Garden	Julie Salter	42
Simplicity	Georgina May Carey	43
My Garden	Heather Dolan	44
An Introduction To Poetry	Natalie Suff	45
Fear Of Nature	John D Savage	46
Summer Dance	Alison Hitch	48
Under A Stone	Kareen Smith	49
The Colours From The Heart's Tender Memory Will Never Fade	Stephen White	50
Men	Hazel Taylor	51
Fairies In The Garden	Margaret Ward	52
Sea Moods	Tony Turner	53
Forest Fire	Philip Walton	54
The Desert	Brian Williams	55
Cow Field	Mike Tracey	56
Landscape	Anne Munro	58
Teatime With Toady	Tracey Tomlinson	59
Earth	Irene Sime	60
March	Brian Mitchell	61
Springtime	Annamaria Pari Fasulo	62
Spring Equinox	Penny Allwright	63
Hah	D Taylor	64
My Poem	Joan Grant	65
Rawtenstall, Lancashire	Mary Braithwaite	66
Sentinel	George Carrick	67
The Angel Of Freedom Waits, At The Dawn Of Peace, In The Garden Of Light	Scott Martin	68
Fairy Games	Ann Blair	69
Spring	Margo	70
Reflection Of Springtime	Lenroy Quashie	71
I'm So Lonely	J M Basey	72
Nature's Riches	Ruth Martin	73
Untitled	Albert Clarke	74

Title	Author	Page
My Sanctuary	Jan Harrison	75
March	Mena H A Faulkner	76
Magic Moments In Corby Woods	Elizabeth Love	77
A Boat's Lament	D Reddick	78
The Butterfly	Samantha Walsh	79
Start Again	Cowguts	80
Wild Daisies	Nayyer Ali	81
Set Me Free	June Swain	82
Spring	Kate Hasson	83
The Lionheart	Boliver	84
The Metal Monster	Daniel McNally	85
Nature's Cathedral	Louise Gardener	86
Bluebells	Helen Baillie	87
A Lancashire Tale	Bill Austin	88
Work Or Leisure?	Jan Patterson	89
Gardening Together	Sheila Killingworth	90
Breakfast	H Morrall	91
In The Garden	E Scott	92
Daytime	Lyn Whitehouse	93
Children From The Earth	Samantha Amy Lawrence	94
Untitled	Hilary Pranskus	95
Into The Garden I Must Go	Isobel Cullen	96
The Gardener	C Beman	97
Against All Odds	S Lee	98
Spiders	Jane Reeves	99
Stand	Michael Turner	100
Like The Leaves That Fall	Trish Downing	101
Hymn To Proserpina	Pearl M Burdock	102
Destiny	Sarah Monaghan	103
Forest Rhapsody	Frank A Zwolinski	104
Storm	Mark L Moulds	105
My Sanctuary	Rebecca Johnson	106
Scandinavian Pine	Andrew Brain	107
Catty Scrat	Barbara Brain	108
Significant Snowdrop	George Smyth	109
The Life Of Spring In Your Garden	Terence Feighan	110
The Rose	James Patrick McGowan	111

Tree Of Life	Andrew Usher David	112
No Sound	Christina Andrea	113
Prey	Robin Tennant	114
The Farmyard	Maureen Ashing	115
Glass Prison	Terry J Powell	116
May	Joy Morton	117
Nature's Whisper	Francis Poet	118
Judgement Day	Patrick Ayton	119
Wonderland Glade	Julie Robinson	120
Life In The Wood	Margaret Rose Taylor	121
Untitled	Edna James	122
The Reality Of Nature	Becky Mason	123
The Seasons	J Sanders	124
Aesthetic	W Robertson	125
Seasons	Susan Hammond	126
Nature	Nikki Burton	127
The Gardener	Panicos Iordanou	128
The Gardener	K Christie	129
Garden Life	Alison Tesloff & Isla Tesloff	130

KILLING NATURE

Fox-hunting and racing is so utterly wrong
It's been killing our nature for so long
Shooting the foxes who know nothing better
Who love our land and the weather when it's wetter

The horses get shot at the end of the game
Don't tell me it's right, it's crazy and insane
The little lambs die straight away
When someone kills them in an absurd way

We need to stand for nature's right
Stop killing our animals it's wrong,
It'll never be right!

Sonya Ogden

THE OAK TREE

Oh precious land where I was born,
as sibling to the wild acorn,
to skylines filled with elk and fawn
and prowling wolves that howled 'til dawn.
With waving arms I reached up high
and spread my leaves out to the sky;
in autumn mists - I watched them die
and fall around me brown and dry.
The bears and boars that foraged round
among my roots spread on the ground,
disturbed a kite - an eagle frowned
and owls flew off without a sound.
A thousand years I watched it all,
as tree by tree began to fall.
The fauna where I stood so tall,
so sadly went to none at all.
The forest glades the ponds, the brooks,
are now just history in books.
Fish all taken by the hooks,
as furs enhanced the ladies' looks.
And so I stand here all bereft,
upon this land where nothing's left,
as men reach out towards the moon,
to find some other land to ruin.

Neil Kelly

THE SANCTUARY

Let me take you to a secret place
that nobody knows exists,
where incandescent flowers bloom
and rambling roses twist.

A place of tranquil serenity
where mind and spirit are one,
with refreshing scented breezes
and a warm, embracing sun.

A place of never-ending birdsong
and sunsets of pure gold,
where all your days can be spent in harmony,
where your body and soul never grows tired or old.

George W Donnellan

CORNFIELD POPPIES

The fields are full of golden corn
Baked in sunlight since early dawn
Under a cloudless sky of blue
See the poppies - a scarlet hue
A brilliant array of wild flowers
Bright and fresh after the showers
Delicate petals of scarlet red
High on stems in the cornfield beds
When the wind blows the field in motion
Alike the sea's tidal oceans
Waves of red and gold appear
Vibrant colours bright and clear
Poppies appear every summertime
When corn grows and the days are fine
There are poppies too on Remembrance Day
For old soldiers who've passed away
Others whose war was won
Years ago since 1921
Scarlet poppies worn with pride
Memories they cannot hide
Pretty flowers wild and free
May you now live in peace.

Sheila Waller

OLIVIA

A hooded figure perched high on roof,
Screeched, 'Aloud! Aloft! Aloof!'
The twilight world in which she waits -
A heart shaped, shrewd, quizzical face.

Dusk, all around her barn top falls -
Time now to quarter churchyard walls.
Hunting ground in gathering gloom -
Overseen by gibbous moon.

Hark! Ghostly echoes across fallen leaves . . .
Winter wind whipping stripped-bare trees.
Harvest mouse scampers through gate -
Unaware of impending fate.

White-feathered breeches propelled off branch -
A merciless launch, from quiet stance.
Arcing wings encloak her prey -
Olivia will hunt another day . . .

Leigh Benton

TULIPS

Have you seen the tulips in borders and in beds,
Standing there like soldiers, holding up proud heads?
They do not seem to mind, when weather is cold and rough,
Although they are so dainty, they must be very tough.

In the loveliest colours, from palest pink to golden brown,
They look like tiny parasols, hanging upside down.
How do they know the proper time, their petals wide to keep,
For just as soon as it is night, they fold them up and sleep.

Soon they will go, but their beauty we will not forget,
We'll think of how they cheered us up,
When the days were cold and wet.

Jean V F Tillett

THE LIKELY LADY

On a mild day after rain
I see the frogs are here again,
Mothers, fathers, sisters, cousins
Crossing the road in tens and dozens
From distant gardens, far beyond
All heading for our goldfish pond.

The young ones hurry through the gate
Quite desperate in case they're late
Whilst oldies find the going tough
And rapidly get out of puff
But know there's room for plenty more
Of course, they've all been here before.

Young Freddy was a likely lad
His flat was called the *Lily Pad*
And at the edge he didn't stop
But jumped in with a bellyflop
Then saw, reclining on a log
This young delicious lady frog.

'Hi darlin',' he croaked with a smile
'I've gotta say I like your style
I'd like to see your mam and dad
And show them I'm a likely lad
I could persuade them both, I'm sure
To have me for a son-in-law.'

'O, come tomorrow, knock and shout,
Mam goes to bingo, dad's off out,
Then you can demonstrate your hop,
That back-flip and the bellyflop.'
They spent the day in froggy bliss
Now she's a Missus, not a Miss.

Stan Whomsley

WALK AROUND

Out for a walk
I slowly go
Especially when I'm feeling low
Just to see what's going on
And what's lying in everyone's lawn

Green grass growing ever so much
People are getting now in a fuss
Trying to get their gardens all done
Just in case we get the sun

I see a frog, a lovely sight
I walk very gently not to give it a fright
But when I come near
It clears out of sight
Like the day which breaks into night

I see a ball
Coming at me
I go around the corner just to see
Two little kids running around
Looking for the ball which can't be found

Leaves in the trees
Are falling down
Without even making a single sound
Hovering about on the dry, cold ground

Papers are flying everywhere
But I'll walk on, oh I don't care
Let them fly high or low
It's not my problem, no, no, no

On a little bit more I go
Just going, going very slow
Wandering about is all I'm doing
Neighbours' gardens are what I'm viewing.

Sharon Fleming

JOHN ON SATURDAY

Oh it's great to be eight and run with the wind
And jump o'er the rushing burn
Then to shin up a tree and breathless see
Where the river makes its turn.
With never a thought for dinner or Mum,
Or for teacher either:
Cos today is free and I'm just me
Don't mention piano either.

All the days of the week when I must be meek
And learn the seven times tables,
And struggle with sums and spelling and such
When I'm neither willing nor able.

Who was it made the days all wrong,
The Saturday short and the weekdays long?
It was adults I bet, maybe even my dad?
I've heard him say, 'Monday, and am I glad!'

The trouble, you see with adults today -
They've made too much work and not enough play!

They've forgotten how long it takes you to see
The pollen and honey sucked out by a bee,
Or to watch a red butterfly dance over the heather,
Or to run from the rain at a break in the weather!

So now it's to school without further delay
And to suffer and wait for next Saturday.

William Hutton

THE LAST WALTZ

Snowflakes dancing,
Twisting, twirling,
Drifting past
My windowpane.
Silent revellers
Deftly spreading
Winter's mantle
Down the lane.

Bright sun beaming,
Snowflakes dying,
Water streaming
Down the lane.
Snowdrops nodding,
Winter melting
Into spring again.

Eirlys Jones

UNTITLED

'Midst winter's gloom, I see a bloom
I stare and then I stop
there in the snow I see it grow
flirtatious little snowdrop.

Then comes the spring, and it will bring
another, trying to focus
upon the earth that gave it birth,
the yellow, purple crocus.

But that's not all, there's one quite tall,
I hadn't lived until
my eyes espied, my heart it sighed,
the yellow daffodil.

In summer's dawn, upon my lawn
I swear they drive me crazy,
the more I mow the more they grow
prolific little daisy.

Beneath the bower, another flower
has banished all my woes
I stand in awe, there's not a flaw
the splendour of the rose.

Like one's first kiss, such perfect bliss
stands one so pure and holy
majestic queen, I'm glad I've seen
the glorious gladioli.

How would it be, to never see
the work of God's creation?
He's made me smile, made life worthwhile
with orchid and carnation.

So I am glad that I have had
the chance to watch God's power
I stand - behold! and see Him mould
another precious flower.

E McCanny

THE WORLD IN A LEAF

The balance of the world is such
A leaf assumes a vital part
In keeping fresh the air we breathe
I thank you leaf with all my heart

The many different shades of green
Then turn to yellow, orange, brown
The leaf in death falls to the ground
To feed next year's arboreal crown

The cycle runs from year to year
With CO_2 absorbed by leaves
And oxygen back in return
Thank God for what the leaf achieves

And yet the trees are still cut down
To clear the ground or for their wood
Which puts the balance of the world
In jeopardy for Man's own good

Of paramount importance is
The cycle of the green, green leaf
The forests must all be preserved
For otherwise defies belief.

David Foreman

DAWN

The morning peeps
to reveal the day,

shards of light
through darkness play.

Ripples on water,
the flap of a wing,

the world waking up,
what a beautiful thing.

J Ellis

BUTTERFALL

Oh! Honest folk on bended knee
Cry aloud at sights you see
Of Astroturf and rubber trees
Painted squirrels, birds and bees
And man, whom pushed so far behind
Machinery that maketh time, stand
And count on weathered hand
Insects from this common land
For progress is to no avail
If upon a single snail
The plastic makes its stand.

Thomas Campbell

RELAXATION

I know the hedge needs clipping
The sun is now so warm
On this lawn I'm kipping
Tall hedges cause no harm.

Poems and rhymes are prancing
Round and round my head
Thoughts and verses lancing
So many left unsaid.

The grass could do with mowing
The footpath needs a sweeping
I'm told these jeans need sewing
But to this spot I'm keeping.

That blackbird now is dining
On titbits he has chopped
Is that a strimmer whining?
Thankfully it's stopped.

Though I'm well intentioned
- Please don't think I'm lazy -
Work I have not mentioned
But work would now be crazy.

Weeding makes me pant
As I'm not fit to race
A weed is just a plant
In the wrong^{ful} place.

Backbone may get tensioned
It's like procrastination
I act like I am pensioned
But it's only relaxation.

Seamus Harrington

THESE ARE THE DAYS IN MY GARDEN

These are the days in my garden, the happiness
These are the days in my garden, the joy,
These are the days in my garden, the peace,
These are the days in my garden in spring.

These are the days in my garden, the wonder
These are the days in my garden, the colour,
These are the days in my garden, the sweetness
These are the days in my garden in summer.

These are the days in my garden, the blossom,
These are the days in my garden, the contours
These are the days in my garden, the contentment
These are the days in my garden in autumn.

These are the days in my garden, of planting
These are the days in my garden, of joy
These are the days in my garden, of short days
These are the days in my garden of winter.

The cycle continues in my garden.
These are the days in my garden.

James McKay

JOBS WORTH

I awake in the morning
And get ready for work,
It's mundane and dirty,
I think, is it worth
All the hours I spend here
Just to earn a few bob?
I wish I could find
A much nicer job.

Then we think of our gardens,
My friend and me,
She says at the weekend
She's planting a tree.
We talk about flowers
Which we have a lust,
It passes the day,
Now this is a must.
But soon the week's over
And now we can spend,
Potting and weeding
For hours on end.

J Shires

BREAKFAST

Hanging nets of fat and seeds,
Coconut shells and peanut strings.
Borders are full of rampant weeds,
Awaiting arrivals on excited wings.

The morning sun has warmed the air,
Now blackbirds, finches, tits, a jay,
Robin, thrushes, sparrows all share
A gargantuan feast, the first of the day.

Attracted now, the neighbour's cat
Arrives to aggravate the fuss.
Birds agree they're not having that
And fly away, leaving disappointed puss.

Margaret Kent

A CHANCE TO SAVE CREATION

Exterior Earth polluted, interior Earth diluted.
Resources are diminished, extinction almost finished.
When will we ever learn, that this world will cease to turn?
If we ignore and do not treat it, its energy becomes depleted.
We are down to our last chance in this evolutionary romance.
It's time for us to heal it, to nurture it and to feel it.
It's given us so very much, food and clothes and such!
We're here to aid with its fruition, it's not a business proposition.
To turn its soil and tend to its garden,
Not sit back and watch it harden.
It's here to teach us a valued lesson,
Yet some of us just keep on guessing.
If we don't learn to listen, and continue to ignore it,
Our ignorance blind, will in turn, destroy it.
So if you love our planet and its cosmic rotation,
Respect its origin, its grace and marvel at its creation.

Jason Alexander Nelson Whitehall

The Oak Tree Is Crying

All my offspring, lay on the floor
this mighty oak, laid bare once more
I weep once a year, for you all to see
standing alone, I hang my sign, let me be
Lady Wind, take my children by the hand
spread them far, far across the land
I will stand and watch you all, sail away
only fate knows, where you all shall lay
but just for a while, let them be
at my feet, to comfort me
I feel the blackbirds' quickening pace,
the rays of the sun, on your face
don't feel sad now, this is how it must be
a mother of Nature, once told me
I feel the wind now children, it's time to go
she will protect you, go with her flow
it's time we parted, even though I'm in pain
the circle of life, is about to start, again.

John Hoyland

UNTITLED

The weekdays are busy and full of stress
So the way to counter this distress
We have discovered a wonderful ploy
Out into the garden and there enjoy
The sights, the effort, the exercise
Culminating in that great prize
Peace of mind and relaxation
Far away the day's frustration
For gardening is such a pleasure
Away go those stresses, worries and pressure
We walk around, sometimes a snip, remove a weed
What more in life could we need?
Than a garden for our leisure
Something we can really treasure
And as sadly we mature
And gain a greater love of nature
The flowers, the trees, the scents, the birds
Something difficult to put into words
Please let this little verse be your guide
You'll never know until you've tried.

John Kingston Pool

ANGEL

Once a time, not long ago
My heart took flight and it was so
That night or day no time would tell
For space would pass, it was not hell

So my heart grew more each day
'Twas a foolish thing I heard you say
I could not see the danger near
If others' thoughts held ever dear

For some can see what we cannot
That life so fragile can be stopped
Our need denied is others' deign
No word or thought must now remain

How to strike the fatal blow
Succumbs the mind from fast to slow
It travels far, to take the thought
Saves conduct becoming as they ought

Then like lightning, truth dawned bright
But it was dark, there was no light
To short the time the angel halt
My mind, my self could find no fault

Life ebbs away, it was too cold
Now bereft of heart and soul
No chance to give that goodbye kiss
No look is given or sigh be missed

And now my angel looks not this way
Nothing I do or think or say
Will change a mind so set on pain
The loneliness left, it will remain

Oh my heart, my life, my being spent
My angel was from Heaven sent
This hurt remains, no words restore
That change will come again to fore

For loved and lost is always said
A better way for all who're led
But far from true as we all know
The sadness that we then have sowed

Then ne'er again, would it be the same
If only angels knew this pain
Like us the hurt and grief to feel
Our love, our life, our peace to steal.

Malcolm Dexter-Tissington

THE BLUE VEIL

Pastel blue shades in June drape down
    from the light in the sky
hiding deep black space from the eye
    touching down on the greenery
covering deep black fenland.

With a sigh I dream of a billion stars
    lost in its hue
when the clear black night sweeps away the thick blue veil
    and folds it around just one setting sun
here is the beauty of the night.

Ten billion floating globes strain their sight
    in the pinpricked glorious night
pondering too the one who made them
    just like you and I
in awe of a nocturnally awakened sky.

Shrouds of day steal
    the night-time beauty from the eye
when the night comes cloudless
    a veil is drawn from the deep black star-struck
ebony light of the night
    touching numberless stars flung to eternity
with my one good eye.

I see the twinkling light of the night
    from a million light years past
drawing me back from the brink of the future
    I go with that one good eye
and see the birth of myriad suns
    one by one over timeless time
just like you and I.

Derek Wade

MY OWN LITTLE WORLD

Golden sunlight kisses all
Unspoken harmony
As a petal gently falls.

A world full of colour
Beautiful silence
A place like no other

Birds build their nests
Delicate balance
Only the best
I feel so at home
Warming comfort
I'm never alone.

Charlotte Willis

GREEN FINGERS?

My lawn is looking patchy, I should be sowing seed,
But every time I do it, the birds have a lovely feed.
Maybe I need a scarecrow, or a line of plastic bags,
I've seen that done on telly and in those gardening mags.
My flowers too are a poor display, withered, droopy, sad.
Yet I water, feed and talk to them (the family thinks I'm mad!)
I put them in lovely coloured pots and stand them in the sun,
So how come nothing grows for me, am I the only one?
They talk about green fingers, well, mine are usually brown,
From digging in the muck and dirt to weed this thankless ground.
There is one place where the grass grows well
And it really makes me sick!
Because, of course, it's on the driveway, even though it's pavier brick!
So Mother Nature, if you're listening, please give me a hand this year,
Let my lawns grow lush and green and persuade the weeds to disappear.
Help my flowers stand tall and proud and wave their scented heads,
Otherwise, I'll lay down my tools and retreat to my garden shed!

Gillian Adair

THE WOOD ANEMONE

In spring the woods are covered
With a carpet, white and green
Of dainty little wind-flowers
The prettiest ever seen.

Each flower has six petals
Pure white, though tinged with pink
The dark green leaves are finely cut
So delicate I think.

Marion Brown

LOOK INTO MY GARDEN

As I sit down and look at my garden I open my mind
To my grand parlour, for this is what my garden means to me.
Oh how much nature has given for all to see.
I watch the birds hover around
As they watch the worms wriggle around,
Oh how happy this makes me.
When flowers awaken from their winter sleep,
Oh how beautiful and radiant they seem to me.
The sky is blue and the clouds are white
And then the sun comes ever so bright.
I look above my garden and see for as far as the eye can see
The green grass for miles around,
Sheep and cows gather to graze all around
But today there is no haze around,
Just butterflies and the bees buzz around,
Oh how happy am I
For today I see a world meant for me
As we can all open our eyes and see,
Just come into my garden with me,
Relax and follow me and let me help you to see what I can see,
For if this world was as happy as me
Oh what an achievement this would be,
For a true celebration of nature and thee,
For this celebration our Father would see.
Oh what a joy this would be.

C A Walsh

A NATURAL MIRAGE

Circling death, smells its own carrion, drifting in the wind. Instinctive law of nature, calls the meek into hiding, rendering subtle camouflage the only versatile weapon.

Beneath the bristling rays of the sun, tunnel feverish survivalists, laying deep the scent of narcotic cultivation, proclaiming Darwin's law, kill burrow, steal.

There are no limits; the wilderness beckons rare, uncompromising and savage. Here none regret the soft cunning of the silent predator.

Flowers open with a beauteous display, inviting all to feast, suspending a delight of carnivorous delicacies, too late to notice the thorn on the rose.

Such elements remain unmanipulated by our human metropolis, disgorging its remnant waste, foraged by those waiting in the shadows to take their meal.

Darren Kelly

A Gardener's Lament

Trays of compost sown with care,
Two months later, nothing there,
Spires of lupins pink and blue,
Clothed in greenfly, not a few!
Plant potatoes, onions, beet,
The bloomin' pests all find so sweet,
And I consistently do fail, to rid my plot of slug and snail.
The weeds I do not plant all grow,
With roots to Australia down below.
I mow the lawn, it starts to rain,
A few days on, it's grown again!
I've dug and raked and sown and planted,
At the dogs and kids I've ranted,
Why do I put myself through this?
Longing for the sun's sweet kiss,
Seeing only rain-soaked skies,
Flower borders like mud pies,
Then hey! The sun begins to shine,
I take it this could be a sign
The hard work hasn't been in vain,
The garden's going to bloom again!

Uldine F Emmerson

DRAGONFLY

Fly, fly dragonfly.
You are so beautiful.
Magnetic.
Start stop, start dart,
You weave desire into your chase.

Fly, fly dragonfly.
You are so purposeful.
Electric.
Blue metallic, blue hues,
You fly on wands of silky lace.

Fly, fly dragonfly.
You are so beautiful.
Fly, fly to me.

L J Liggett

Untitled

I had a pretty path
Outside of my little house
In a rural place
Which had high hedges.
I planted over time
Space became all full
Colourful shapes
Foxgloves, honeysuckle, herbs, mint,
Fuchsias, sweet peas, lilies, roses.
As I passed, they touched me
By skin vision inside my heart,
Smelling so lovely,
Such a divine, lingering scent.

Sue Norris

The Gardener

The gardener is busily preparing the ground,
Digging nutrients, and enriching the soil, all round;
Planting tubers, corms and bulbs, for seasonal display,
The daffodils, hyacinths and primroses in glorious array;
Wisteria clinging to the house, with the ivy covering the gables,
The vegetable plot full of onion sets, turnips, and parsnips, in neat rows,
The paper bows crossed-over, to deter starlings and crows;
Runner beans and peapods, herbs for good health, which richly pays,
Luscious raspberries and strawberries, planted for summer days;
Rhubarb crowns for those delicious crumbles and tarts, for the table;
The apple, pear and apricot saplings, are fastened to their stakes,
Nearby, amongst the wheelbarrow, garden tools and the rakes;
The lawn is mown and aerated, re-seeded and watered,
Seeds are sown, in autumn, for next season, are now evenly quartered;
The hedges have been cut, and designed into unusual-angled joins,
The art of topiary, in contemporary designs of spheres, birds and
                                                               noble lions;
Marble statues of the Venus de Milo and Adonis, adorn the
                                                                landscaped splendour,
With the water feature invoking peaceful serenity close to the arbour.

Irene Greenan

PENDLE

Majestic and dappled, dark mists lifting.
This hill as usual its mood shifting.
Crones and bones of yesteryear.
Tales of superstition, foreboding and fear.
The Nick of Pendle, stories of witches.
In the daylight of summer the landscape switches.
To springs and streams gushing and flowing.
Wild flowers, the bowers, natural beauty showing.

The birds fly, the deer graze ever so near.
What do they know of foreboding and fear?
Spring lambs on the hill gambolling and lazing.
Cattle in the fields contentedly gazing.
Young animals in general suckling on mother.
Knock-kneed unsteady, trusting no other.
Jackdaws and magpies swooping in the fields.
Searching and scavenging for the food that it yields.

The sparrow hawk soars and hovers.
Never a thought for the prey it bothers.
Rolling hillocks of light emerald green.
Panoramic views just aching to be seen.
A secret garden, no I think not.
This hill holds secrets better forgot.
Crones and bones of yesteryear.
Tales of superstition, foreboding and fear.

Ellen Spiring

FLOWERS

As the morning sun came up from the dark
With a light mist in the park
Not a soul around or even any sound
Imagine as the daylight broke
Mist is starting to life
I'm writing this, what a special gift
Never before would I write a poem,
Just wandered home
Flowers full of colour blooming in their pots
Yellow daffodil, red, red rose
And lots of lovely marigolds
Pushing through the ground quietly, without a sound
As I walk with no one to talk to, or even smile
This road goes for miles and miles
But I still find a smile for a while
When I see that girl
The day has ended, going back home
Along the way I stop to look at the pots
Of forget-me-nots, their cups starting to close
Like the daylight turning to dark
As I return through the park.

David Williamson

HARVEST TIME

It was a lovely autumn day
The stems of ripened corn did sway
Gently in the breeze.
Their golden ears slightly bent
As if they had a presentiment
They had only another day's lease.

The combine harvester soon came along
To cut and sort out many a ton
Of this golden treasure.
The granaries were filled to the top
Then tired men into seats would flop,
Give thanks and have some leisure.

The Lord be praised in all the land
Who blessed us so we may not want,
Who's everlasting kindness
We never can extol enough,
Give thanks that He shows us such love
God grant, we'll never be mindless.

Joan-Ing Reed

A Fairyland Of Bliss

A fairyland, a fairyland, a fairyland of bliss
To wake next dawn or early morn
It seemed the world had been kissed
The hillsides and the valleys so gaily adorned

The Lord had put on a mantle
Of crisp, shimmering, glistening snow
And reminded us that our winter
Had quite a while to go

The children happy and delighted
To play their games of snow
Building snowmen, having fights
Until their fingers really glow

Until now the winter has been moderately mild
And I'm going to tell you this
That if it does not change it will be
A fairyland, a fairyland, a fairyland of bliss.

Iorwerth Thomas (Miner's Poet)

SILENT DREAM

Today a little child was born
With wrinkled face and head quite bald.
It kicked and cried, bewilderment set in its eyes.
The mother all but a child herself, looked down
And what she thought, no one could tell.
She held the child up to her face
And kissed it gently and with grace,
She then lay back quite free from pain,
She never saw her child again.

A wise old lady died today
Her face quite wrinkled, her hair quite grey.
There were no kicks and cries.
And no bewilderment in her eyes.
She had known where she was going
And she had known where she had been,
She had had a full and happy life,
She had lived her mother's dream.
For yesterday, when she had been young,
The world had been hers, to her it had belonged.

Dorothy Ellis

SPRINGTIME

What could be more beautiful
than a woodland in the spring,
with noble bowers of ivied oak
from which the blackbirds sing?
Eager tongues of April sun
caress the dew-soaked ground,
fresh from sleep a startled fox
is gone with just one bound.
Newly spun, a spider's web
brightly shimmers in the breeze,
silken threads bedecked with jewels
dripping gently from the trees.
Wild flowers all around,
God's paintbox must be dry,
not so the tinkling pebbled brook,
as it flows sweetly by.
With cruel barbs the brambles grow,
amongst the ferns of lace,
shyly from a clump of briars
a dog-rose shows its face.
Gently zephyrs stroke the trees,
their whispers seem to say,
what could be more beautiful
than a woodland springtime day?

Jim Cruickshank

MY GARDEN

I really love my garden at the closing of the day,
The perfume of the roses as I wander on my way.
Each flower a different colour, from red to blue, then grey,
My garden is a peaceful place where I can sit and pray.
A haven for the children, it is where they like to play,
The washing blowing on the line, the lawn in disarray,
Sandwiches and biscuits and lemonade on a tray,
But I really love my garden at the closing of the day.

Julie Salter

SIMPLICITY

I love the ocean, I love the sky,
I love the gypsies, I love simplicity,
Like leather and lace,
And the rain and snow,
The things we take for granted so.

If I had my way I would live with my love
In a far off land;
Where greediness doesn't flow,
And where God's creations still come alive,
Every day and every night.

People are always running,
Never really knowing where they are going to;
Society builds these boxes, that you must stay in and do;
It's like living in a world run by narrow minds and not the sky,
And the only ones that remain are the true gypsies.

They are the poets of the world,
Who just live for the sunrise;
They know not of hate, but only how to love more.
With their horses and carts and their magical crystal eyes,
They stay up at night to praise the moon and she looks down on them,
Relieved they still remain . . .
Making their own way . . .

Georgina May Carey

My Garden

As I go into my garden and look around
I marvel at the beautiful flowers I've found.
The smell, the colours, the sight and sound
Is my garden colours all around.

I look around and the colours are mixed
The seeds I have planted, a rainbow is fixed.
I look around and see how time has passed,
How things have grown, how things have passed.
I will pull and prune and feed and grow
To let the garden colours show.

As I look around and wonder
Will I be able to plant another border?
The rain will come, the sun will shine,
The seasons change in this garden of mine.
I will toil the soil and start again
And remember the rainbow in my mind.
Reds and yellows, pinks and greens
Are the seasons of colours that are all to be seen.

Heather Dolan

AN INTRODUCTION TO POETRY

Creation is a great way to start
It's the beginning with a better name
But to write from the depths of your very heart
Is more often a difficult game
To happen is to think
It startles to be inspired
Something that comes as fast as a blink
Leaving one quite tired
Imagination is the key to all things
From bright ideas to dreams
So intense it plucks your heart strings

So here comes the introduction to poetry
A mystery
A gift that comes from the soul
Priceless, as it only comes naturally
From days of old
When told by mouth, flowing like a zephyr
The magic of words gets better
Intricate sketches of sounds
Imprinted on Mother Nature
A vibration of waves that travel around
Its beauty endures, lures

There are no rules for making words
It's like teaching a bird to sing
It cannot learn until it's heard
From elders wise and old
Language is a strange thing
Delicate, precise and told
From word, to poem, to song
A story concealed within
In mystery few unfold
But life goes on
In patterns and rhymes . . . that's poetry.

Natalie Suff

Fear Of Nature

The jagged air gasped me from my breath,
As my hands clasped fretfully together,
I could taste the dew upon the grass vaporise on my tongue,
My eyes were fixed steadily full of fear, his were of a remote calmness.
He slogged forward like a beast,
His muscular shoulders powered his legs,
As all four worked in motion, his head lurched up and down,
His slobbery tongue clobbered his lips.
I shuddered like a little mouse afraid of a cat,
My body was frail and fragile, unworthy of competition against him,
I saw an opening, of which I ran into.
The wind impaled against my face like sharp daggers of wrath,
As I battled across the field, to which it was empty,
I didn't turn around, I was full of fear.
A burning ambition captivated my mind,
An ambition to face my fear, I would return someday,
To which he would fear me.
I saw it before, a shiny, sharp point, with the plastic body on the end,
A syringe they called it, I saw how they pitched it in,
And how the beast would get frisky, as it banged into the metal bars.
He was in my territory, he should fear me,
He stood still, to which he could go nowhere,
The rusty bars forming a crush,
Separated us.
I pulled the syringe and placed it in the air,
As though I was a warrior with a sword,
I felt powerful and mighty, he was a weakling,
Remembering of how I felt when we first met.
He feared me, like I feared him.

His eyes crossed with mine, he was full of repulsion,
I was full of calmness,
To him I was the beast.
I pulled the syringe down, my embracing hand let it fall to the ground.
I now feared myself, and feared
What I can accomplish.

John D Savage

SUMMER DANCE

Busy people in the midday sun
Saturday market
Spoiled for choice
Children whizzing
Whirling around
Ice cream faces
Summer dance.

Busy people in the midday sun
Bells ringing
Confetti thrown
Children hopping
Laughing out loud
Foolish talk
Summer dance.

Busy people in the midday sun
Hand in hand
Strolling along
Children tiring
Sleepy eyes
Summer days
Summer song.

Alison Hitch

UNDER A STONE

In the dark under a stone
a centipede lived all alone.
He would walk the garden
when all the sounds were lessened

But when he heard my trampling feet
he would make a speedy retreat
back to his nest under the stone
where he is now not all alone

For he has the company of another
it is either wife or brother
for surely in time I will tell
if the population does indeed swell

whether he has found a companion
in a centipede's marriage union.

Kareen Smith

THE COLOURS FROM THE HEART'S TENDER MEMORY WILL NEVER FADE

The calm majestic evening cloud
Lying gently in its pastel hoists,
Casts through the cotton distance
Greeting more worlds than I could know,
From here is truly mine.

The first drop of a golden aperitif
To the most full and sharing
Of Earth's four wild feasts
To which I may bring five
Though will be given enough for a lifetime made.
The colours from the heart's tender memory will never fade.

Stephen White

MEN

Men are very complex creatures
With unusual charms
And some peculiar features
Getting to know them
Can take years and years
Sometimes cause many tears
But if a good one you should find
Remember to keep this in mind
The man in the boy
May be hard to conceive
But the boy in the man
May be hard to retrieve.

Hazel Taylor

FAIRIES IN THE GARDEN

Listen, can you hear them
The fairies in the grass?
If you listen carefully
You'll surely hear them laugh
Come and play, they chatter
It's lovely in the beds
The aroma of the flowers
Flowing around our heads
The tulips and the daffodils
All are out in bloom
The garden's coming alive
Buds and blossom too
The pond is waking up
Goldfish waking from their sleep
The waterfall is flowing, so the fairies wash their feet
Oh come and have a splash, it's time that we did meet
So if you're feeling down
In the garden you must go
Join in the frolics of the fairies
All wanting to put on a show.

Margaret Ward

SEA MOODS

The sea can be mighty, ever so strong
Crashing and pounding, whilst doing its wrong
Caring not for the damage it does
As it turns about on its daily trudge.

The sea can be gentle, ever so calm
Lapping and rolling, not doing any harm
People bathe while children play
As it flows on its peaceful way.

The sea has many a different face
Never will it be put in its place
Take it from me, a sailor of old
Who's been in its midst when angry and cold.

So whatever its mood, if you should meet
Its strength and power you will not beat.

Tony Turner

FOREST FIRE

I walk through a landscape of darkened wood,
Ebony tears, gently flowing like blood.
Landscape scenery burnt all around
A deafening silence, a chilling, ghostly sound.

A smouldering landscape, beauty burnt to its knees,
Deadly quiet shattered by naturalists' pleas.
Colours all faded, no wildlife to be found.
Today's deserted ruins, was yesterday their playground.

Destruction, devastation in a lifeless zone.
A place of once beauty, reduced to one tone.
Of blackened ash, of cinders and char,
Where columns of colour, once grew tall and spread far.

An eerie mist hangs down from the sky,
As smoke-filled clouds gently breeze by.
A picturesque painting, burnt to the ground,
No colours of beauty, only black to be found.

Forest life, burnt, drained and bled,
From its living veins, the fire was fed.
Its vampirish flames, hungered for blood,
Leaving this forest of darkened wood.

Philip Walton

THE DESERT

Sun beating down on barren parched land
Lizards and spiders hide in the sand
Dried wizened plants dotted about
Stunted from growth because of the drought.
Rats in their burrows stay out of sight
Nervously waiting for the safety of night.
Side-winding snakes glide over the land
Arching their backs from the heat of the sand.
Scorpions hide under rocks all the day
Patiently waiting for some passing prey.

Waterholes dusty from the sun's intense glow
Gnarled and contorted, a tree struggles to grow.
The haze in the distance makes the sand shimmer
The way that it looks, it could be a big river.
Heat unrelenting day after day
An eagle is circling, hunting for prey.
A vulture is perched in a tree on its own
Waiting to strip the meat from the bone.

Constantly trying to escape from the sun
Looking for water, but there is none.
Mother and calf wander about
They are both very weak now because of the drought.
Away in the distance thunder claps roar
At first it starts slowly, then rain starts to pour.
Like a great curtain it sweeps over the land
Bouncing off rocks and soaking the sand.
Waterholes fill up, animals drink
Some time in the desert and life on the brink.

Brian Williams

Cow Field

On a bright and sunny day
To the cow field I make my way
My two dogs for company
And today we wonder what we may see?

Grass green, wavy and tall
A loud buzzing noise from insects so small
Squawking from magpies starting a fight
Dive bombing, chasing a buzzard in flight.

Rabbits graze in peace very unaware
They smell the dogs and suddenly they are not there
Without warning, crashing from the undergrowth on my right
Four deer charge past me, an amazing sight.

Trees and thick fern grow all around
A blanket of yellow and blue covers the ground
Clamber over wire fence, steep hill I climb
To a resting place, which is mine.

For here to sit and think thoughts in peace
Brings inner calm along with stress relief
Clear blue sky with sunshine on my face
It's great to drop out of that rat race.

But alas, cannot stay forever here on my own
The dogs are restless and it's time for home
Must leave this cow field with its abundance of life
Walk back to the world, family and wife.

Breathe in deep, let out a contented sigh
I feel a bit itchy; I wonder why?
Standing up to leave this place
The look of contentment leaves my face.

For company has found me out
I jump, leap, and give a shout
What an end to a perfect day
Sat in an ants' nest, to my dismay.

Mike Tracey

LANDSCAPE

I am the waterfall tumbling from a great height
As I cascade down the rock face I'm an impressive sight
I am the pool catching it every day
Then over pebbles and stones I go on my way.

We are the trees, in the wind we do sigh
As we raise our heads proudly to the sky
I am the field where cattle, sheep graze and lambs they do play
My sister next door resplendent in hay.

I am the desert of golden sand
Hot and barren in this humid land
I am the ocean shining blue
Teeming with life that's hidden from view.

We are the flowers with colours so gay
Together we make a lovely bouquet
I am the sun with golden ray
Bringing warmth to the earth today.

I am the rain, cold and wet
But I'm needed as well don't forget
I am the snow, fluffy and light
Covering all in my path with a mantle of white.

We are God's creatures of earth, sky and sea
Fish, birds, animals, butterfly and bee
We too are part of this hemisphere
We live our lives year after year.

We are the seasons, summer, autumn, winter and spring
A different view to surroundings is what we bring
We make the scenery for all to share
Put all of this together and landscape is there.

Anne Munro

TEATIME WITH TOADY

We alter the clocks tonight
Light nights and weather bright
It makes you feel better
Go for a walk around with our Irish setter
God's been good, we should be grateful
In His trust we should for ever be faithful
Everything's starting to sprout
Months behind closed doors tightly shut
One problem is who's going out for logs
And coal for the fire
Nice and cosy, all you could desire
You put the kettle on, I'll do it
Toad's on the back having a swim
No he's not, he's just walked in
So there he's sat
Lovely, brown and fat.
What do you feed toads?
Grubs and worms, you silly p**t
He's not a cat
You can't give him a saucer of milk
I do worry about you sometimes
Off he goes, his skin is so cold
By the way he's told me
He does not like the disinfectant you use
You worry about me, I think you're getting old
Who would talk to a toad
What's your excuse?
I'd better put the kettle on
Are you sure he does not like tea?
For heaven's sake, please believe me.

Tracey Tomlinson

EARTH

Dry, dusty, unyielding
Wet, chocolaty velvet
Nature's unsung wonder
A dark, mysterious womb
To beauty!

Outwardly quiet and dull
Keeping untold secrets
Of incredible power
Of dogged perseverance
Of beauty!

Strongly comforting in smell
Taken for granted
Who really cares
For the ultimate wrap
Masking beauty!

Such clever understatement
So complex, quietly nurturing
A song to be sung
Coming alive in spring
With beauty!

A prison in winter
To some dark enclosure
It then helps them fight
To freedom and splendour
And beauty!

Irene Sime

MARCH

Half-past the hour
Of snowdrop droop
And crocus curl,
With snow confined
In freckled cornices,
When daffodils go trumpeting
Their yellow voluntary,
Whilst bread-and-cheese
Buds green between black thorns;
Forsythia gilds suburban gardens,
Overhanging ponds
Where frogs spawn sago pudding,
Spiny urchins,
Fresh from hibernation,
Crunch spiral shell accompaniment
To blackbird song,
And pussy-willows
Kitten catkins
Under skeletons of trees,
Embroidering a new layette
For coming spring.

Brian Mitchell

SPRINGTIME

Butterflies' wings growing on trees
With premature fruits, naked the sun
Is covered by clouds' brim and,
The wind makes laugh the leaves . . .

Brisk arms of pale petals
Waken up with kid's first smile
In gardens' sleepy houses,
In an early warmth
Of an earlier springtime . . .

Annamaria Pari Fasulo

SPRING EQUINOX

Upon the equinox I stand and look out at the view
And past the daffodils, the cherry plum has changed its hue.
From winter black, in February its brilliant blossom shone.
The scent attracted bumblebees but with the frosts they'd gone.

March came and so the flowerless tree stood black through gales
                                                          and rain
'Til this day, looking out, I see that it is green again.
Its tiny leaves unfurled at last, the nest box can't be seen.
It won't be long before the other trees are turning green.

The birch is still in winter grey, the catkins you can see,
And apple, ash and elder buds have not yet broken free.
But in my garden, cherry plum is first of all of these,
With early blossom and first leaves, my favourite of trees.

Penny Allwright

HAH

Look at that little bird
It has a silly grin.
Wonder where it's bin?

Oh dear, I do fear,
Pussy's got it in its mouth.
My wife will think I am a lout,
If I don't go and get it out.

As I headed for the door,
I slipped on something on the floor.
Through the doorway I did go,
Landing on the pussy, so,

If you see a little bird
Singing in the rain,
It's singing about a pussycat
That will never be the same.

D Taylor

MY POEM

Nature has a funny way
Of having its say.
When the sun peeps through
The bulbs in the ground say, 'Me too.'
Once bleak and bare
Growth happens without a care.
First a mass of white.
Snowdrops, what a welcome sight.
A few weeks pass,
Be patient, my lass,
Beautiful, bright, yellow stars,
Daffodils have graced us as if from Mars.
More bursts of colour,
Purple, white and yellow,
Nothing here is mellow.
Caring crocuses blanket the ground,
Oh, I think a piece of Heaven I've found.

Joan Grant

RAWTENSTALL, LANCASHIRE

In Rawtenstall
the bracken hills climb high
with tumbling green valleys.

The hills tumble,
the trees and the heather
into the valleys
of greens of light and deep.
Flashes here and there
of yellow gorse.

The little houses huddle.
The air is cool and clear
thrilling me with rareness.

I love the place.
To be alone
free as a gull
in the early morning sky.

Lovely as snowing
these valleys and hills.

Mary Braithwaite

SENTINEL

Silver leaves with forest bark
Doth nature seed,
The slender waving willow keen
To intercede.
Emerging growth as springtime offers
Succour from its trees,
Ever ripened and freshened
On the gentle breeze.
The wily fox, silent and still,
A sentinel savage yet unseen,
Watches life erupt, as creatures stir,
And wake from dreams.
Fleeting shadows flicker
As a warren's young arise,
And the silent sentry strikes,
As savagery greets sunrise.

George Carrick

The Angel Of Freedom Waits, At The Dawn Of Peace, In The Garden Of Light

Her garden is always green
The flowers, eternally, in bloom,
The blossoms' sweet perfume
In rainbows of light, are seen.

Many yearn to visit her, there
Many more have waited, in vain
Others, lost in their despair, have
At the end, breathed her name.

For her garden was always green
For all eternity, if we could only see,
Sweet peace and freedom for our race
She turns to show her kind, fair face.
In the garden of light,
The most beautiful bloom
Is a tapestry, woven upon the loom.

The threads are justice, the harvest is peace
If we could but see it,
All war will cease.

Scott Martin

Fairy Games

Down at the end of the garden
Hidden under the rustling trees
The fairies don't ask any pardon
Of the busy bumbling bees

Hidden under the rustling trees
The fairies play and frolic with permission
Of the busy bumbling bees
When the rain is in remission

The fairies play and frolic with permission
Chasing through the flowers and leaves
When the rain is in remission
Using rose petals to make tiny sleeves

Chasing through the flowers and leaves
The fairies don't ask any pardon
Using rose petals to make tiny sleeves
Down at the end of the garden.

Ann Blair

Spring

Sleeping quietly underground
Waiting for spring to come around
Nature's flowers will appear
Rising through the ground so bare
Showing colours of every hue
Purple, blue, to name a few
Reminding us that spring is here
Giving hope for future year
No money can provide
Nature's wonders that abide.

Margo

REFLECTION OF SPRINGTIME

The exit of winter comes the entrance of spring
Hey sparrow! Is that my song you sing?

The flower beds paint with colours quite rare
As butterflies admire, some even stare.

Trees that once lay bare
Again blossoms to share.

The warmth of spring flushes the covered snow,
Delicious fruits from blossoms grow.

Blackbirds, have you tasted nectar so sweet?
But from distant lands, you must retreat.

The stiffened earth stirs gently from the rain of spring
And within swampy ditches, hungry crocodiles grin.

Across green fields, homeless cows graze,
As the scent of fresh dung lingers in outer space.

Oh bending immortelles that bathe beside the stream,
Or attractive daffodils, who lift their dresses to tease.

To the rose garden, watch how the fork digs,
See scissors cut, to remodel your beauty before season ends.

Lenroy Quashie

I'm So Lonely

How could you hurt me?
I can't believe you couldn't see,
You've made me feel so lonely,
I thought I was your one and only.

You say, 'You used to moan and moan,'
You hated me speaking to my friends on the phone,
Is that why you've left me all alone?
In this cold, damp flat I call home.

Did I ever treat you right?
We used to always fight,
But those fights always ended with a kiss,
That kiss is what I will always miss.

What did I do wrong?
We were together for so long,
I gave you all my love and devotion,
It was as deep as the deepest ocean.

You've shattered my heart,
That's because you wanted us to part,
I really thought I was your one and only,
But instead, you've made me feel ever so lonely.

J M Basey

NATURE'S RICHES
(Psalm 104)

When the sun reaches its zenith in the sky,
And the moon and stars illumine the black of night.
When dewdrops sequin the green blade,
And the spider weaves her lacy orb.
When buds burst forth and blossom fruits,
And buzzing bees and trilling birds flit and fly.
When silver-bellied fishes leap the gushing stream,
And white mute swans grace the stillness of the lake.
When summer rains precede the rainbow arch
And gentle breezes disturb the leafy bough.
When fields turn golden with the corn
And coloured flowers labyrinth the grassy sod.
When nature's riches stir the heart of Man,
How can we say there is no God?

Ruth Martin

Untitled

Towards the changing colours
Of many flowers in bloom
There is a start to spring
That will become in tune

In and out of the garden
Along the grass before
Beneath the colours of flowers
And there are many more.

Albert Clarke

MY SANCTUARY

my garden, my escape
my sanctuary
after the trauma of the day
to sit at sunset
watching birds dancing
in the sky
and the pond
as skaters glide across
damselflies
of blue and green
oh such total peace
such utter tranquillity
like nothing else matters
just this nature at play
when it thinks no one
is watching
how I adore this time
my time
just me and nature
the deep red sky
and never-ending peace
my garden, my escape
my sanctuary.

Jan Harrison

MARCH

'For lo, winter is past,' sings Solomon
But our March remains grim.
The month of expiation,
Roman purification,
So let us prepare for spring.

March may come in like a king,
Acting out its Goliath bluster,
Martius, the month of Mars,
Ancient Roman god of wars
Set on forces to muster.

But gentle April stands by in the wings
Like a city that needed no sun
As God's glory brightened
And the Lamb's presence lightened,
The dark winter's race had been run.

Mena H A Faulkner

MAGIC MOMENTS IN CORBY WOODS

I have a favourite place in Corby Woods
Where I return to every year,
Where the path leads onto a promontory,
Three tall oaks on the river's edge,
Veil the sky with their delicate green
Lichen and ivy-covered
And on the overhanging boughs
The dancing light of ripples plays
There is one of those rare rhododendrons
Large and bell-shaped and deep red.

Where I sit,
A bearded monk stands guard over the centuries,
Children play on the flat stones opposite,
Ringed by marigolds,
And far above their heads come echoes
From the Wetheral caves.

'Is there anybody there?' the children shout.
'Only Mr Wolf,' comes the reply,
While round my feet
The ants weave in and out the debris of another season.
A bee, a wasp, a butterfly,
The everlasting chant of birdsong,
The movement of the water,
They have always been the same
In this enchanted place.

Elizabeth Love

A Boat's Lament

I'm fifty
And I know I'm in my prime
I meander through this England
To help me fill the time.

From York
Right down to Oxford
And all the towns between,
I think you'd be amazed
At all the things I'd seen.

With geese and swans and kingfishers
A truly wondrous sight.
I travel 'neath the warm day sun
And then the stars by night.

I've been out sixteen months,
I've been through every season.
From spring when all the flowers pop
To winter when it's freezin'.

My name is 'Grandma Scruff'
They say I'm like my sister.
My hull is made of English steel
But my heart was made by Lister.

D Reddick

THE BUTTERFLY

You opened your wings,
A wonderful sight,
A spectrum of colour,
A joyous delight.

A beautiful creature,
So happy and free,
No problems or worries,
I wish it was me.

You hovered and fluttered
And danced all around,
Then, no . . . without warning,
You fell to the ground.

I thought about life,
How you live and you die,
This beautiful creature
No longer would fly.

No longer so happy,
No longer so free,
This unhappy creature
Reminds me of me.

Samantha Walsh

START AGAIN

Out comes the sun to shine
And here come the better times
With hope renewed
From sour winter
As spring makes us feel better

See glory in all around
As birds sing their sweet sound
And life begins
We can start again
As with nature, we make friends.

Cowguts

WILD DAISIES

Wild daisies, so soon they haste away
Little fancy linger your transient stay
The grass is greener because of you
The more it enchants, the more you grow
Enclose within yourself to shun
The harsh sunburn
Separate awhile but only when
If you promise to return again.

Nayyer Ali

SET ME FREE

Set me free with the wind,
Where trees go unshinned,
In dells where bee dips,
And butterfly flits,
Let me find my home,
I dislike being so far, so alone,
Set me free on the mountains,
With the fountains
Of streams
Running through like silvery seams,
Where green trees blow.

Let me go
And taste the rain,
Feel the wind and no pain,
With pretty flowers at my feet,
There I could sleep,
I wish to shake
This old, aching, flesh and bone,
Don't leave me alone,
Leave me in the forest
Where I can rest
Under green tree,
Set me free.

June Swain

SPRING

Reclaiming winter's barren scorn
Reaching dark corners
A new direction of light - stretching
Calling men of soil

Love thrust upon challenging forces
Opening earth's frosted crust
Revealing precious jewels
Delicate in their form - protected

Its coming presence will yield
Bringing forth new seeds
A thousand fold - nourished
Planned summer love - sighing
Continuing its cycle.

Kate Hasson

THE LIONHEART

Not far removed from maternal breast
Wide blue eyes vacant with thought
So young and knowingly free
Always vigilant, always on the watch
Thro' garden she'll slyly stalk
Seeing every move of leaf and tree
Guardian and protector of her patch
With purpose and meaning in her walk
No lion be this, but a kitten she,
Who will boldly fight and scratch
To make the return to the feline nest.

Boliver

THE METAL MONSTER

Once I stood so straight and tall,
Now you humans have made me fall.
The rabbits ran around their burrow,
Now they sob for love and sorrow.
The goldfinch perched high in my tree,
It now will have to flee.
The blossoms on my branch had started to bloom,
I watched the squirrel as he would groom.
The monster came out from the grass,
It was made from metal, machinery and glass.
The monster opened its mouth and cut me down,
My mother and father gave an awful frown.
It started to chew me,
I fell down to one knee.
Now I am a bedside chest,
Inside me only one vest.

Daniel McNally (10)

NATURE'S CATHEDRAL

As I walk through a woodland glade,
I marvel at the creation God has made,
A carpet of sapphire to be found
As bluebells cover woodland ground,
Emerging paths then appear,
At the end stands proud a deer,
Listening for danger, but not in fear,
With the sound of a bird's wing will disappear,
Trees stand strong and tall,
Green-leaved branches shade bluebells small,
Standing still, looking high,
Leaves dapple clear blue sky,
Choir of birds, sweet and clear,
Was the only sound while sat here,
Nature's cathedral, there's no better place
To retreat from the human race.

Louise Gardener

BLUEBELLS

Have you ever walked through a bluebell wood,
And been struck by a mass of blue?
To fill your lungs with that delicate scent
In the early morning dew?
This little bell, so perfectly formed,
Moving gently in the breeze,
Protected from the elements
By the sturdy, old oak trees.
This lonely wood so peaceful and still,
Never a footprint to see,
Only the rustle of a wandering deer
Roaming so wild and so free.
I sit in the shade of this beautiful glade,
I think about winter and snow,
Whatever nature bestows on this land,
This tiny bluebell will grow.

Helen Baillie

A Lancashire Tale

Lil' Molly were a weaver,
    In the days of cotton's boom.
But to see her and believe her,
    Too small to run a loom.
Her knees felt like they'd buckle,
    But she had to do her bit
And continue 'kissing t'shuttle'
    With Father hurt in t'pit.
Since Mother went to live with God,
    She'd to feed her siblings too,
Each morn to t'mill she had to plod
    And work at what she knew.
Now Jacob used to tackle t'loom
    And took a shine t'weaver,
A feeling which was common soon,
    He found it hard to leave her.
There was no room in Molly's life
    For 'coortin' or to wed,
He couldn't take her for his wife
    So he'd steal a kiss instead.
Time went by, and t'siblings grew,
    And Father joined the mother;
The lovers made their plans anew,
    For each one loved the other.
With the talk of marriage topical,
    And fruition on its way,
A honeymoon spent tropical,
    They're a Darby and Joan today!

Bill Austin

Work Or Leisure?

Now that spring is in the air
Daylight comes quite early
The weather's not quite at its best
Requiring me to wear a vest.

However this morning was brighter
I dressed in something 'au fait'
Hurried through my breakfast
And started on my way.

A good brisk walk to start my day
For work was calling me
But no one else was there about
A 'natural phenomenon' to see!

Yes, at least that's what it seemed
As each new step I took
The path was strewn with earthworms
'Where's my fishing hook?'

Big ones, small ones, short and slim
Each step along the way
There were lots and lots of them
Should I work or should I play?

Jan Patterson

GARDENING TOGETHER

We work together a few moments at most
Because I tend to wander from pillar to post
He works with precision and stays in one spot
Because he is the expert and I am not.

When friends come round to admire and visit
They look with envy and say, 'How is it
Your crops look well, and your lawn is green,
Whilst ours is bare, and pickings are lean?

What do you do to enrich the soil?'
I smile and say, 'With sweat and toil.
With silent prayer and lots of luck,
But most of all, plenty of muck.'

Tired and weary at the end of the day
I've worked well under supervision, he will say,
But nevertheless it's always the same
When things go wrong, I get the blame.

Sheila Killingworth

BREAKFAST

I look out my window
And what do I see?
A couple of chaffinch
Come out of the tree
They've come for their breakfast
Of nuts and wild seed
But are soon chased away
When blue tits come feed
The robin arrives for
His share of food
But the fieldfare appears
To be in a mood
He frightens the others
Until they are gone
At this moment in time
We have none.

H Morrall

IN THE GARDEN

Sitting in my garden
Watching my husband cut the grass
I say to myself, never mind,
My hay fever will pass.
Then into the garden comes next door's cat,
The only time he moves is this time of day,
But only to use my garden as his litter tray.
I hear the buzz of a bumblebee,
Has he come for my flowers?
No, he comes straight for me.
As I lay my head back, I hear the birds sing,
It takes my mind off my throbbing bee sting.
By this time both eyes and nose are runny
And what with the swollen bee sting,
I do look funny.
But no matter what I look like,
I'm really pleased to say,
It's nice to sit in the garden
On a lovely summer's day.

E Scott

DAYTIME

Sitting in the conservatory wondering what to do next,
Glancing at the Garden News I came across your text.
I will put pen to paper and see how I fare,
I'll give most things a go, I like a bit of a dare.

The flowers in my garden, they do look a super sight,
Planting took forever but it seems I've got it right.
Nodding brightly at me on such a cold spring day,
All the hard work was worthwhile, what more can I say?

Robins are at the bird table sifting through their food,
Nearby blue tits have been nesting and are busy with their brood.
Mr Squirrel will appear very soon with no manners whatsoever,
Digging up the nuts he buried and looking for his treasure.

April showers have now passed over, a golden sun is in the sky,
Steam is rising from the garden bench, soon all will be clean and dry.
Time to stir myself and think ahead of chores that must be done,
I have enjoyed these last few minutes, it's been a lot of fun.

Lyn Whitehouse

CHILDREN FROM THE EARTH

I laid my children in the ground,
They filled the many holes I found.
I threw a cover over them,
Whilst they slept with a compost hem.
They woke up in the days to come,
And I felt as if I was their mum.
At first they only dared to peer,
Until they knew the sun was near.
Their hands reached for the guiding beams,
For they knew this was their only means,
To pull their sleepy neck,
Up from the compost deck.
I see them now standing tall,
Knowing they will no longer fall.
They cling to a home down in the earth,
To which I know they owe their birth.
Now my children need me not,
To find a hole or fill their pot.

Samantha Amy Lawrence

UNTITLED

A fairy lives in my garden
You'd never know she's there
But she spreads a little magic
For everyone to share
I find her footprints in the clover
And hear her singing with the birds
The contentment she sprinkles in my garden
Can never be put into words
She spreads calmness amongst the ladybirds
And causes havoc with the bees
If you look a little closer, you'll see the leaves move
As she flits high up in the trees
She's very clean my fairy, she often has a shower
I feel the dampness in the air
And smell her perfume on the flowers
She's very good with a paintbrush
She must paint the plants at night
Cos first thing in the morning
Gosh, what a beautiful sight
When I sit here in my garden
Oh what joy she brings
I'm surrounded by her beauty
She's left it on everything
She's left it in the borders, the tubs and baskets too
She's made me love my garden
I love it, through and through
I never believed in fairies
But now I'm sure they're true
And if you look closely in your garden
You'll find you've probably got one too.

Hilary Pranskus

INTO THE GARDEN I MUST GO

The springtime days, becoming longer,
The sun intense and much stronger,
Beseeching me out to join with the birds
Serenading with song, but never a word.
Picking up the sticks to build their nest,
Working so hard, completely obsessed.

The grass is cut and looking well,
Perceive the sensation and the smell.
Disturbing the ground, the robins having fun
Eating the worms as up they come.
Showing how it's done to the next generation,
As it's been done, since time and creation.

Trimming the grass and raking it back,
Rotating the earth, I've got the knack
Of weeding, weeding and weeding,
And planting out last year's seeding.
It will be worth it in the end
To be seated in the garden with my friend.

Already the sun is burning my back,
At twelve o'clock I'll have a snack,
With tea or coffee, certainly a drink,
Will give me loads of time to think.
Sitting under a tree in my favourite chair,
Enjoying my lunch in the clear fresh air.

Isobel Cullen

The Gardener

As winter passes with the start of spring
And birds in the trees start to sing
The crocus and daffodil start to flower
A garden job beckons for every hour
From dawn to the last daylight
Even beyond and under false light
Our labour we start to deploy
But a time we greatly enjoy
With digging the veg plot and planning done
Thinking of the meals we have to come
On bad days I sow flower seeds
Always too many for my needs
When small plants start to emerge
I feel my adrenalin start to surge
With the vegetables, herbs and flowers
Taking up many unpaid hours
Hard labour I sometimes need to deploy
With an achievement feeling I really enjoy
Great pleasure I get as I plod on
Laughs also come as things go wrong
When bad weather tries to spoil my fun
Jobs like potting up can be done
After cutting the lawn and raking out moss
And chasing off cats that dare to cross
Plants shaped and pruned one by one
The weeding, watering and feeding all done
I share my garden with the birds and bees
And people passing by it seems to please
Then as the summer sun starts to shine
My garden matures like a rich, sparkling wine.

C Beman

AGAINST ALL ODDS

April rain
A planting moon
Hail again!
Spoke too soon . . .

Gardeners cope
With wind and showers
Work and hope
For summer flowers.

Come the sun
We take heart
This is fun
Can't wait to start!

S Lee

SPIDERS

Dandelions and daisies pulled up out of bed
In come the daffodils and roses of bright red

Weeds are laid to rest
So the garden can fully bloom
We don't want the dandelions, we simply have no room.

The ants will build their nests
And the spiders spin a web
As the sun gets warmer, the insects lay their eggs.

But we don't notice them and only the pretty flowers
Feeding hungrily off the sun for hour upon hour
Then the pitter-patter raindrops fall to quench their thirst
Lots of moisture stored in the dry, crumbling earth.

Seasons come and go
And the leaves will start to wilt
No consideration for our efforts
The seasons have no guilt.

So while we wait another year
The spiders come inside
But be careful what you move, as you may find where they hide.

Jane Reeves

STAND

When I crawled inside a pain, it seemed I had to bear,
I saw trouble, understand it was not mine.
When a moment's thought could sum, you left me standing there,
For burden I was ill prepared this time.

Where a hope should grow there stood a solitary low
And a mind that occupied this empty throne.
At the sunlight's end you're waiting, whispers tell me so
They remind, that when we stand, we stand alone.

Michael Turner

LIKE THE LEAVES THAT FALL

Like the leaves that fall in the winter of our lives,
We too, grow to give flower in our personality.
Tend to fall when rejected.
Sadly our bloom is not as long as our nature.
Surely we should treasure ourselves more?

Trish Downing

HYMN TO PROSERPINA

She's here once more: her touch we see
Illuminates the Earth;
Brings magic to last season's tree -
Eliminating dearth.
The silent goddess strikes again
Inspiring seeds to grow -
With recreation. Spring's refrain:
New life unfolds its glow.

In times gone by: mythology
(Before Christ lived and died)
Would need no great apology;
Belief in gods applied.
Belief in what they saw each year
In nature's miracle;
For certainty they could adhere
To wise man's oracle.

This goddess kisses majesty
In many shades of green;
Embracing life's tranquillity -
Exquisite sights are seen.
Demeter is her mother; she's
The goddess of the grain,
And Zeus (chief god of Heaven) sees
To sun, the wind and rain.

In bringing forth all nature's world;
The excellence in life.
In winter's dark, dead leaves lie curled;
She lives as Hades' wife.
When we say 'Mother Nature's spring'
And speak of 'Father Time'
Perhaps it's Proserpina's fling;
Rejoicing, free, sublime.

Pearl M Burdock

DESTINY

The sea was royal and enchanting
As it melted into tiny twinkling pebbles
Loved and left by the waves
Who entice the gems further - further away
Into a sea of unknown.
Like gentlemen escorting ladies at a ball
They dance and swirl around them.
The dazzling sand beneath thy feet was brusque.
Brusque, sturdy, feminist, yet nearer the charming waves
It was weak and easily led,
Led easily into a sea of unknown . . .

Sarah Monaghan

FOREST RHAPSODY

The magic charm unfolds
and Pandora's box spills darkened coloured glories
into the unknown: forty shades of tinted greens
which appease and soften the stilted
myopic vision.

The rooftop canopy of leafy boughs precludes the gleaming
kaleidoscopic rays of nature's celestial light,
casting eerie shapes, rendering mystique and fear to
creation's dank and musty garden: where Adam fathered sinful fruits.

From the spongy brown shag-piled forest floor
sporadic clusters of yellow primroses
give pitiful flickering light to the vast
unlit palace of God's glory.

Calm and fear collide in confrontation, but
expectant hesitancy fires a burning curiosity
to explore the depths of tantalising
smells and sounds.

Outwith visual context a contrapuntal litany of
thin discordant sounds choruses awareness
of flora and fauna: of the dancing trees
rubbing shoulders in disharmony with the embalmed
leaves and twigs protesting the intrusion of man and beast.

The Aeolian wind-section crescendos the full
orchestral forest cacophony to double fort!
But what of the shady, leafy woodland, reflecting
the elegiac glories of Gray and the romances of Wordsworth?
This can only be the well-worn and threadbare path
to the unfinished symphony of no-man's-land.

Frank A Zwolinski

STORM

High in the oak the stormcock sings
A warning borne on zephyr's wings,
An anvil head of leaden cloud
Chills the air beneath its shroud.
Rain in silver lances pound,
No creature heard above the sound
As stream and river ride the flood,
Transfused with Earth's life-giving blood.
A maelstrom forged in gold and green,
Nature's anger reigns supreme,
Old timbers groan in disbelief,
Their roots torn out like aching teeth.
This mystic earthbound passion spent
Its wild embrace is onward sent,
And in the oak the blackbird sings
His joy at what fair weather brings.

Mark L Moulds

MY SANCTUARY

As I step outside and feel fresh air on my face,
I realise I only feel peace in this wonderful place.

It's my heaven in a world
that I fail to understand.
This simple heaven is contained
in a small, square piece of land.

The simple orange tulips
stand to attention on their stems,
the snakes' had fritillary
carpeting the cordyline hems.

The Cornish-bred narcissi
bought on a blissful honeymoon,
pale and peaceful, yet so poised,
even the primula turn to swoon.

Buds on spring flowering clematis
prepare to burst into flame; my
anticipating building, of more colour
in a corner quite tame.

Even when passing fading hyacinths
in their limp and tatty guise,
nostrils fill with such sweet perfume,
I'm constantly taken by surprise.

It's such surprises and beauty,
helped by Mother Nature's hand,
that keep me going in a world
that I fail to understand.

This heaven, this sanctuary, all in
my small, square piece of land.

Rebecca Johnson

SCANDINAVIAN PINE

Regimented to a fault
Silent our new forest grows
It takes in CO2 and stuff
But doesn't seem quite real enough
Treated, sprayed and canopied
To keep off acid rain, you see
Forgive me if I think it's strange
That they're geometrically arranged

Residents all up in arms
About an eco offshore farm
That makes electric from the wind
Guess they could plug John Prescott in
Protestors on the evening news
They say it spoils the lovely view
It seems to me the choice is clear
Offshore wind or just more nuclear
Let me hug you now - Scandinavian pine
Tell me all your secrets and I'll tell you mine
To the Gaia whole from a rootless man
There must be some room in between all of their plans

The devil's in the detail boys
Like who this logging firm employs
With dubious legality
Cheap labour to fell a tree
Long hours on the gang today
Breaking backs for pittance pay
Migrant workers out of doors
Wondering what they came here for.

Andrew Brain

CATTY SCRAT

Where's that primrose that I planted?
Ooh - what's that squiggly thing there?
Oh - that's the root.
One upturned primrose I do declare.
Dig another hole and plant it again,
surrounding it with steadying grit.
Next morn I go out again. What's happened now?
My primrose looks wilted. Sad, dejected one.
your head should be to the sun, not terra firma.
Bird, have you been tugging at its leaves?
Or has Tom next door used it as its tray
passing through this joint
peeing on my plants, raising up its rear
in a haughty toilet dance?
Will it live or will it die?
I'm thinking that a prayer is needed.
My hands reach out to the ceiling,
'Oh Lord, please make my primrose grow,
I would have liked it for a show.'
Super squirter - here I come!
Watch out cat, I'll splash your bum.
That orange feline scrounger
has used my lawn as a sun-lounger.
Not only that, but the blasted cat
scrats his holes and rolls and rolls
and tugs and plays and then runs away
as soon as my steps are heard.
Shooter in hand - I fired at will
but failed to fill
and nothing came out but hot air.

Barbara Brain

SIGNIFICANT SNOWDROP

Suddenly they appear,
the advance party of spring.
Here to spy out the land
like a host of witnesses
draped in white.
Hundreds of bell-like petals,
sturdy for their size,
standing shoulder to shoulder,
resisting the pouring rain.

Suddenly they appear
announcing to the garden,
'Colourful days to come.'
Soon the crocuses will bloom,
but for now
pure white is in abundance.
Opening batsmen,
certain to make an impact,
swaying the balance to spring.

George Smyth

THE LIFE OF SPRING IN YOUR GARDEN

As you sit in your garden
Admiring the beautiful flowers
Starting to grow in your garden
And other people's too,
You know spring is here
And the sun shining down
So brightly from the sky.

As you're looking inside your
Beautiful spring garden,
You see little baby birds flying
With their mothers into your garden
And they know spring is here
As they learn to fly.

You know spring is here in your garden,
The rain comes down and washes
Your beautiful flowers away,
That you planted a long time ago
With a bit of help and care from God's hands,
You know spring is here.

Terence Feighan

THE ROSE

Achoo, achoo, *achoo!*
Why, why, *why?*
A flower. A flower. *A flower!*
With *hay fever!*

Yes I have - how pathetic,
Those dirty grasses
With their filthy pollen
Just make me *sneeze!*

Achoo, achoo, *achoo!*
Ooh a bee, please, please.
Itch my nose, itch.
Ah my saviour, tell your friends.

So please Mr Gardener
With all your sprays and feed,
Give me something to stop my . . .
Aaaccchhhoooo!

James Patrick McGowan

TREE OF LIFE

Plant a seed in the ground
see how much it grows.
Nurture and water,
sunlight and space,
give it time to show.

Winter, summer and spring,
pain, happiness and love
each will bring.

Autumn time there is nothing there,
the leaves, the tree
no longer bears.

The tree, although as
tall as the sky,
it is now time
for the tree to wither and die.

Andrew Usher David

No Sound

Soft tipped velvety grass, swaying,
Each blade in time with the other
Hearing an unsung melody.
With fragrant blossoms, lavender trees
Sprinkle blooms - adding to the melodic feel
Like tinkling piano keys.
Fuchsia bushes' trumpets of cerise
Nod along, creating a splash of colour
In an otherwise pastel shaded garden.
Blackbird hopping along the hedge
With a shush of percussion
As it rustles stiff leaves.
Sun's golden orb - high in the sky
Radiates its warmth
Smooth . . . dreamy liquid gold,
No sound - none required.

Christina Andrea

PREY

Over Medwynn Moss now open and bare,
the silent hunter on electric perch
awaits small movements in the marshes.

Foreign fields, familiar sun,
graceful gliding hides fatal intent.
Eye and claw in unison steeled.

Then, rising back through the morning mist,
talons grip their gory haul. Nature's balance
takes its toll. To the victor, the spoil.

Robin Tennant

The Farmyard

Dusty lane!
Grinding mill
Open barn
Farm machinery
Higgledy piggledy
Horse's head over gate
Sultry sweet smell of calves
Slobbering as they munch at hay
One licks a child's arm
Making him squeal and squirm
Black and white cows
Plodding from the milking shed
Ducks and geese
In murky pond
Musky and dank
Acrid and rank
As they dive and play
Hens pecking in the dust
Yellow chicks at their heels
A collie dog in the sun
Tabby cats sit
Watching for mice
Honey-laden bees
Returning to the hive
The drone of a bumblebee
Ambling idly by
Time to sit and dream
Relaxing in the sun.

Maureen Ashing

GLASS PRISON

In my prison made of glass
Trapped inside a transparent mass
No corners to hide your fear
Cylindrical, dome-shaped, and clear
Shouts resound the echoes inside
But silent deafness of mime outside
Strong and cold inside your silicone wall
Escapeless to one and all
Impregnable in all its might
Illusive to trap and holds all its light
Crystal, clean, and clinical
Pure, and cynical
I am looking out, as they look in
With nowhere to go, they know where I've been
I see them pass by in my crystal dome
In this incarceration I call home
One tiny chip is all it takes
Before this structure breaks
Just to make a tiny flaw
Shattering it to billions of tiny shards, to make it fall
To breathe the air of freedom once again
But here in this see-through fortress, I remain
And they still look in, as I look out
No corners to hide my fears and doubt
I see them walk by and pass
In my prison made of glass.

Terry J Powell

MAY

Summer's usher, Celtic Beltane,
bonfire-burning harbinger of the beauty to come.

May-flowering, white hawthorn,
fertility-promising preserver of arboreal spirits.

Procreative powers hurried homewards
in arborescent armfuls:
as tree-touching respect is rewarded
by future good fortune.

In symbolic sacrifice
of youthful innocence,
dancers encircle
the majesty of May's pole.

Joy Morton

NATURE'S WHISPER

Like the sound of the wind
Through the willow trees,
That distant hum of the honey bees,
Radiant sunshine bright and warm,
Watching the swallows so swift as a storm.

Grazing, enjoying the landscape's delights,
Fields of corn, birds in flight,
The sweet smell of flowers wild and fresh,
A smile to my face filled with happiness.

Escaping to a world where worries cease,
Sunlight rains down on cattle and sheep,
Horses run wild with pride as they canter,
Visions of delight to all they encounter.

Pretty blue flowers wild in their bloom,
Growing in places searching for room,
The rustle of the bushes like a secret hush,
The silence is quenched by the stillness of it all.

Francis Poet

JUDGEMENT DAY
(Dedicated to Lorna my mum. Love Paddy)

My day of reckoning is here
A day to truly fear
I've thrown it all away; I've made some bad choices
I've done some things I shouldn't have done,
I've pulled myself out of so many holes
Only to make the same mistake again
And end up in the cold
To turn back time is not an option
The reaper's at the door
I can't stay - he's here for me - I don't think we can talk anymore
I'll try to hide but we both know
That I haven't got long left
My time is up and my day is here
And that's what I've got to accept.

When there is no forgiveness for our sins
When the sun that shines so bright begins to dim
When the life from our bodies begins to stray,
The day we fear is Judgement Day.

Patrick Ayton

WONDERLAND GLADE

Creeping canopies of smoky lace
envelop the leafy glade.
Spectre-like fingers dripping with dew
sweep across the trees leaving victims wet with soaking brew.

Followers are adorned in see-through gowns
embroidered with blob-like pearls.
They dance and tease around each tree
washing the forest in dewy whirls.

Once more the wonderland glade returns to life!
As the sun's rays bathe it in torch-like light
illuminates each tree reflecting lights
of every hue - as if from a magic wand.

Julie Robinson

LIFE IN THE WOOD

There's oak, ash and many a tree
Standing erect for all to see
Scot's pine, silver birch, holly too
Horse chestnut and elm, just to mention a few
Fir cones and acorns lie scattered around
On a cushion of leaf-mould gently covering the ground
In odd little corners and crevices close by
Are toadstools and fungi looking forlorn and shy
Bluebells, anemones and red campion grow
Primrose and foxglove all give a show
Briars and nettles make their presence known
Next to the ferns that stand all alone
The birds sing their praises - oh what a life
Free from all traffic, worry and strife
Wood pigeons, jays and carrion crows
Perch along branches in neat little rows
Blackbirds, thrushes and linnets all come
To join in the chorus of the woodpecker's drum
The squirrel stays close with his artistic skill
Performing his tricks that capture and thrill
While dear little rabbits peep out from their burrows
Looking for food in clearings and furrows
Foxes and badgers stay well out of sight
Venturing out with the dark of the night
Honeysuckle scent and a gentle waft of sweet columbine
Make life in the wood so rapturously divine.

Margaret Rose Taylor

UNTITLED

The path that leads upwards
May seem rocky at times
But the sun always shines brighter
The higher it climbs.

Edna James

THE REALITY OF NATURE

Paw prints tracked across untouched snow
Wolf pack running, ghostly figures
Front runners, eye to eye, no sound
A silent communication.

Across the stream they dive and swim
Straining towards the bank ahead
For one the swim demands too much
His weak old legs can stand no more.

Left on the bank, forlorn and lonely
To face nature's reality
The harshness of the wild alone
Will find him out and beat him down.

At last his ending moment comes
Head, heavy fall onto the snow
Pink tongue touches ice-cold blanket
Wise eyes, tight shut, the final time.

Ahead the pack give hunting call
Following deer thin and starving
For one to live, another must die
Living wild, enforcement of law.

Hidden from yelping pack below
A mother wolf in wooded den
Warned with a growl her two young cubs
To be as silent as they could.

Many laws of nature hated
Of life and death, and death and birth
Most harsh, all unavoidable
All part of life for creatures wild.

Becky Mason

The Seasons

Spring is a time for a new beginning
The flowers are blooming, the birds are singing.

Summer is a time for holidays and sunshine
Barbecues in the garden, and having a good time.

Autumn is time for leaves a-turning
Harvest gathering, grass fires burning.

Winter is a time for rain and snow
Long dark nights, and fires aglow.

The festive Yuletide is a special season
Although shorter, it has a reason

A time for families and friends to be together
Caring and sharing, whatever the weather.

Another year ends and the seasons start over
Also, of course, we are another year older.

As the world goes round and times do change
The seasons, thankfully, remain the same.

J Sanders

AESTHETIC

Blessed they the mighty dead
Who from this life they now hath fled,
Their monuments may still remain
With written works to entertain:

And painting works of ancient arts
Enough to fill a thousand carts,
Medals, titles, downward cast
Without life, they never last.

Blessed too are those with none,
Whose sands of life are still to run,
They still remain and there be free
Unhurried to eternity.

W Robertson

SEASONS

Spring

'Hug a tree,' they said.
Enfolding the smooth beech bark
I can hear the spring.

Summer

The smell of roses
Delights the summer days
And moth-soft nights.

Autumn

The first frost pinches
Fallen leaves collect in rustling drifts;
A robin sings again.

Winter

Beeches are at rest
Smooth grey columns blend with mist,
Wet leaves lie silent.

Susan Hammond

NATURE

In a world full of uncertainty,
All around us still we see
The magical beauty of nature, running wild and growing free.
Flowers are in bloom and gardeners excite,
As we look on in awe and marvel and delight

Each day is filled with trials and tribulations,
Laughter, tears and cause for celebrations

We fill our lives with material and insignificant things
Rather than revelling in the magnificent wonder nature brings.

Pretty flowers, green meadows, woodlands, forests and lakes
Bright sunshine, strong winds, rain downpours and snowflakes.

Nothing is for certain in this world that we live
Each day is taken for granted but there's so much more we can give.

Our families, our friends and the love that we share
Good health and happiness to this nothing can compare.

But treasure and adore both life and nature
For these are gifts given by God the Creator!

Nikki Burton

The Gardener

Green as grass the fingertips
That tended seeds with watery sips
And patiently awaited bloom
Of opulence from nature's loom
Time poured forth its ebbing sands
As craft flowed free from skilful hands
Working under watchful gaze
Of eyes made wise by many days
Buds and blossoms new, pristine
Rising slowly, young and green
Delighted birth of life unfold
As youthful as their maker old
Then full bloom royal, gold and gleaming
Majesty of life when teeming
Calling forth a spirit weary
Eyes aglaze a moment teary
But then a smile did curl the lips
Of one with greengrass fingertips
Set to pass as work is done
The rest of time in summer's sun

Panicos Iordanou

THE GARDENER

How happy is the gardener
When he's in the potting shed
Nurturing the new born seeds
That will make the flower bed

He will plant the little seedlings
With tender care and love
And watch them as they start to grow
From the sunshine up above

And when the flowers start blooming
They'll be picked to bring some cheer
And brighten up a weary life
Until they bloom again next year

K Christie

GARDEN LIFE

Down in the garden the plants grow fast
Until the summer months are past
Pretty flowers standing bright
Sunrays giving extra light
Sweet scent of new mown grass
I hope this summer lasts and lasts

Alison Tesloff & Isla Tesloff (9)

INFORMATION

We hope you have enjoyed reading this book - and that you will continue to enjoy it in the coming years.

If you like reading and writing poetry drop us a line, or give us a call, and we'll send you a free information pack.

Alternatively if you would like to order further copies of this book or any of our other titles, then please give us a call or log onto our website at www.forwardpress.co.uk

Anchor Books Information
Remus House
Coltsfoot Drive
Peterborough
PE2 9JX
(01733) 898102